ANARCH

Crawling Cockroaches

by Robin Nelson

first step nonfiction

Lerner Publications ◆ Minneapolis

LERNER

SOURCE

Expand learning beyond the printed book. Download free, complementary educational resources for this book from our website, www.lerneresource.com.

The images in this book are used with the permission of: © Preiselbeere/Wikimedia Commons (CC BY-SA 2.0 DE), p. 4; Dorling Kindersley/Universal Images Group/Newscom, p. 5; © iStockphoto.com/sabrettep, p. 6; © Bates Littlehales/National Geographic/Getty Images, p. 7; © Paul Starosta/Corbis, p. 8; © Heinonlein/Wikimedia Commons (CC BY-SA 4.0), p. 9; © Minden Pictures/SuperStock, pp. 10, 11; © Rod Williams/naturepl.com, p. 12; © Marka/SuperStock, p. 13; © Olivier Parent/Alamy, p. 14; © Ardea/Pat Morris/Animals Animals, p. 15; Stephen Dalton/Minden Pictures/Newscom, p. 16; © Nigel Cattlin/Alamy, p. 17; © Graphic Science/Alamy, p. 18; © iStockphoto.com/photographereddie, p. 19; © David M Dennis/Animals Animals, p. 20; © Donald Specker/Animals Animals, p. 21; © iStockphoto.com/Antagain, p. 22.
Front cover: © Drew Avery/flickr.com (CC BY 2.0).

Main body text set in ITC Avant Garde Gothic Std Medium 21/25.
Typeface provided by International Typeface Corp.

Lerner Publications Company
A division of Lerner Publishing Group, Inc.
241 First Avenue North
Minneapolis, MN 55401 USA

For reading levels and more information, look up this title at www.lernerbooks.com.

Library of Congress Cataloging-in-Publication Data

Names: Nelson, Robin, 1971– author.
Title: Crawling cockroaches / by Robin Nelson.
Description: Minneapolis : Lerner Publications, [2016] | Series: First step nonfiction. Backyard critters | Audience: Ages 5–8. | Audience: K to grade 3. | Includes index.
Identifiers: LCCN 2015041871| ISBN 9781512408812 (lb : alk. paper) | ISBN 9781512412192 (pb : alk. paper) | ISBN 9781512410006 (eb pdf)
Subjects: LCSH: Cockroaches—Juvenile literature.
Classification: LCC QL505.5 .N45 2016 | DDC 595.7/28—dc23
LC record available at http://lccn.loc.gov/2015041871

Manufactured in the United States of America
1 – CG – 7/15/16

Table of Contents

Cockroach Bodies 4

Where to Find Cockroaches 12

Food 16

What Cockroaches Do 19

Cockroach Parts 22

Glossary 23

Index 24

Cockroach Bodies

Cockroaches are large insects with flat, **oval** bodies.

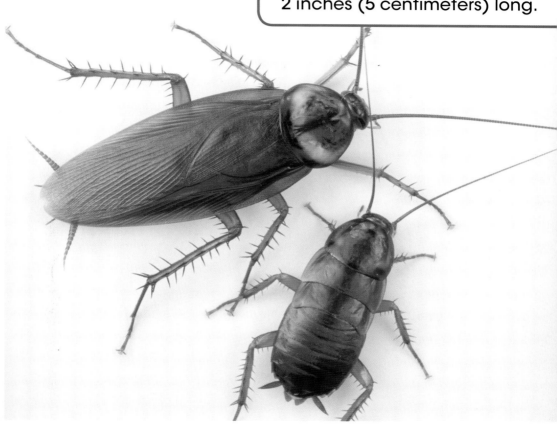

Cockroaches can grow to be 2 inches (5 centimeters) long.

Their bodies have a hard **shell**.

They can be black, brown,
or reddish brown.

Some cockroaches cannot fly.

Most cockroaches have wings.

Cockroaches have six
long legs.

Their legs help them run fast.

Cockroaches have two **antennae**.

They use their antennae to
find their way in the dark.

Where to Find Cockroaches

Most cockroaches live in warm forest areas.

Cockroaches sometimes live in basements.

Some live in **damp**, dark places inside buildings.

13

Cockroaches crawl through pipes and cracks in walls.

Cockroaches are often on the hunt for food.

They look for places that have food to eat.

Cockroaches hide during the day and eat at night.

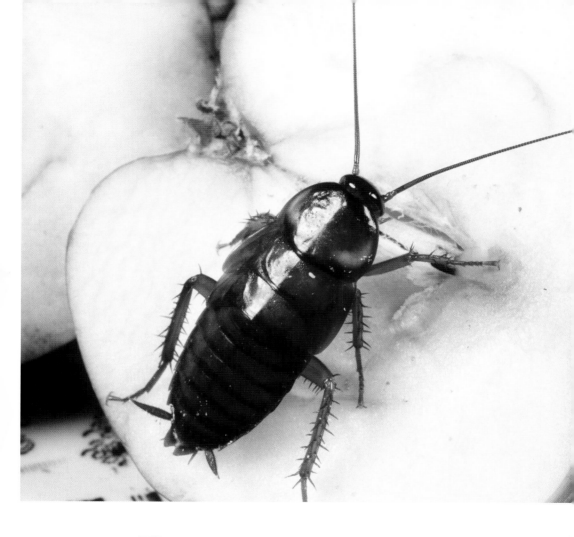

They will eat almost anything.

Two cockroaches eat food scraps.

Cockroaches might eat food scraps, dead insects, paper, or clothing.

Cockroaches live and eat in groups.

They tell one another where
to find food.

If you see one, there will
be more!

Cockroach Parts

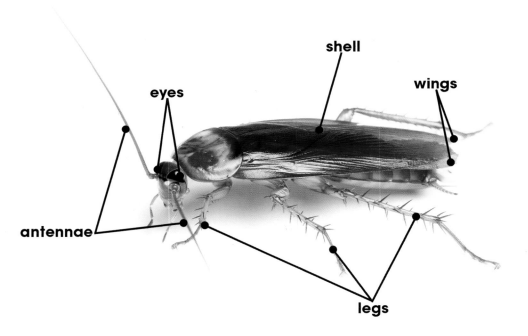

shell

wings

eyes

antennae

legs

Glossary

antennae – long, thin parts on the head of an insect

damp – slightly wet

oval – having the shape of an egg

shell – a hard outer covering on an insect

Index

antennae – 10–11, 22

legs – 8–9, 22

shell – 5, 22

wings – 7, 22